Queen City Adventure

by Emma Latier

Elmira, New York
January 1 - December 31, 1902

New York History Review Press
Elmira, New York

Queen City Adventure
by Emma Latier, 1902
transcribed by Diane Janowski

Copyright © 2010 Diane Janowski
Published by New York History Review Press
Elmira, New York

Notice of Rights. All rights reserved. No part of this book may be reproduced or transmitted in any form by any means, electronic, mechanical, photocopying, recording or otherwise, without the prior written permission of the author. For more information on getting permission for reprints and excerpts, contact us through our website.
www.NewYorkHistoryReview.com

For the latest on New York History Review, please visit
www.NewYorkHistoryReview.com

Front cover image: East Water Street in Elmira, New York postcard published by The Valentine & Sons Co., New York.

Back cover image: small image found in the pocket of Emma Latier's diary

ISBN: 978-0-578-06938-8

First Edition
Printed in the United States of America

For Floyd

- So much to be thankful for -

Table of Contents

Foreward..8

People in this Diary..12

Maps of Elmira and area..................................15

Queen City Adventure......................................17

Afterward..93

Bibiliography..94

Foreword

In our *Learning from History* series of Upstate New York diaries, accounts of young people's lives on the farm, or in the home, help us to understand their thoughts and experiences. Each narrative offers a unique perspective on young peoples' lives in rural New York, and serves as an important primary resource in the study of American history.

Queen City Adventure is the journal of 26-year-old Mrs. Emma Knapp Latier during 1902 in Elmira, New York. Emma Laura Knapp was born on April 3, 1876 in Wayne, New York. She married Floyd Latier on her birthday in 1895, and they moved to Elmira, where Floyd was a bookkeeper for the Standard Oil Company. They lived at 551 East Church Street.

Beginning on January 1, 1902, Emma recorded the events of her life in a small 6 x 3⅛ inch pocket diary with three entries to the page in very nice handwriting. Emma's notations were confined to the spaces allotted and were always written in pencil. Her handwriting is mostly legible, except for a few names or places that cannot be deciphered. Emma's spelling is left as she spelled it. Any clarifications have been added in brackets. The photographed pages from her diary are actual size.

Emma had many good friends and neighbors back home in Wayne and in her new town Elmira. She was very happy in her life and enjoyed her husband, family, friends, and club activities. Often times friends and family travelled to Elmira by train to visit. Elmira was a grand place in 1902 with upscale shops, the opera and theatre, fun activities at Eldridge Park and Rorick's Glen, and fine restaurants. The population was 35,000 and rising. Elmira was also a main hub for the Northern & Central, Erie, and Pennsylvania railroads. Trains came and went in all directions. In 1851, Harpers *New York*

& Erie Railroad Guide gave Elmira the nickname "Queen City of the Southern Tier." A line in their book reads:

This is the queen city along the New York & Erie Railroad and is a good specimen of the towns that seem to exhale from the American soil.

Queen City Adventure invites us into the daily life of a young woman in upstate New York in her own words and experiences. We hear Emma's voice as she shares her life in the "big city."

The Eleanor Barnes Library acquired Emma Latier's diary in 2010. So far as is known, this transcription is its first published version.

Diane Janowski, Publisher
New York History Review

A postcard view of the corner of West Church and Walnut Streets. Publisher Hugh C. Leighton, Portland, ME.

People in this Diary
Emma's family in 1902

Floyd Latier - husband, age 26, bookkeeper at Standard Oil Company, Elmira
Marceus Adelbert Knapp - father, age 51, vineyardist/farmer, Wayne, NY
Mary Knapp - mother, age 47, Wayne, NY
Philetus W. Latier - Floyd's father, postmaster of Grove Springs, NY
Melissa Latier - Floyd's mother, Grove Springs, NY
Carrie Latier – sisiter-in-law(?) lived in Elmira(?)
Brothers - John, age 16 (he came to visit in Elmira); "the boys" Oliver, age 13; George, age 9

Relatives and friends

Aunt Lydia
Aunt Emma
Uncle Dan
Aunt Jennie & Leon
Aunt Sate Knapp Stowell
Frank Ashcroft/Ashcraft - Jefferson County(?)
Phoebe Bailey - lived in/near Grove Springs, NY
Frank Berner - grocer
Miss Biddleman
Mrs. Bodworth
Mrs. Cora Brown - lived at 555 East Church Street, Elmira, lodger
Lelia Brown - age 21, lived at 306 Dewitt Street, Elmira
Katie Bruedich Burdick
Arch Campbell - age 30
Mrs. J.W. Cleveland - Wayne, NY
Mr. & Mrs. Cole
May Covert - Grove Springs, NY
Will Covill
Miss Covill
Mr. & Mrs. Cramer
Lula Dale
Mr. & Mrs. Embleu or Eublem
Esther

Mr. Farr
Mr. Farris
Mr. Ganutz
Lizzie Geiger - dressmaker
Louise Geiger - age 53, lived at 655 Lake Street, Elmira
Charles Glover - age 39, traveling salesman
Grace
Mrs. Hancock
Mrs. Heller
Mrs. Ina
Jim
Mr. & Mrs. J. Johnson
Mrs. Jones
Will Joralemon - Wayne, NY
Bee K
Lillian Katzmann
Satie Kiefer - Grove Springs, NY
Lizzie & Grace, Lizzie & Mrs. T
Supt. Maloney
Mr. & Mrs. Mathews
John & Carrie Mathews - lived at 605 East Church Street, Elmira
Calvin McKinney
Sanford & Cora Messinger - lived at 555 East Church Street, Elmira
Leon Murdock - Wayne, NY(?)
Dr. & Mrs. Noble - lived at 410 East Church Street, Elmira
Marie Noble
Mabel & Josie - Elmira College girls [?]
Maybelle/Mabel P
Mrs. Lena? Paltrowitz -age 32, lived at 459 East Second Street, Elmira
Minnie Paltrowitz
Clinton and Cora Paul
Mrs. Nichols
Dan Quinlan - actor, lived at 206 Washington Avenue, Elmira
Mr. Read - picture framer
Mrs. Riggs & daughter
Florence Riggs
Mrs. Roby

Carrie S
Mrs. Searles – lived at 503 West Clinton Street, Elmira
Mildred Shaw – age 17, lived at 424 West Third Street, Elmira
Ray Shoemaker
Mrs. Floyd Shoemaker - Grove Springs, NY
Mr. & Mrs. Slater
Mrs. Cark Smith
Ray & A Stapleton
William Starbird – age 40, bookkeeper, lived at 612 Park Place, Elmira
Rufus & Mary Stowell & Lizzie - lived at 503 East Church Street, Elmira
Mrs. Stratton
Mrs. F. Sunderlin - age 30, lived at 225 Brand Street, Elmira
Mrs. T---p—
Ella & George Taylor - lived at 112 East Second, Elmira – George was an auditor, age 25; Ella [Eleanor] age 19
Mrs. VanNorts
Mr. Waller
Mrs. Winkle – milliner(?)
Mrs. June W
Belle W
Mr. [Reinhold] Warlich – Russian musician, lived at 406 Union Place, Elmira
George Waters – artist with art gallery at 313 East Water Street, Elmira
Bill & Mr. Webber
Mrs. Webber
Lottie Webster – dressmaker(?)
Mrs. Weigan
Mrs. Weygant Wayne
Mrs. Whitman
Mr. & Mrs. Whitmore
Mrs. Wilson

West Water Street. Publisher: C.S. Woolworth & Co., Elmira, NY.

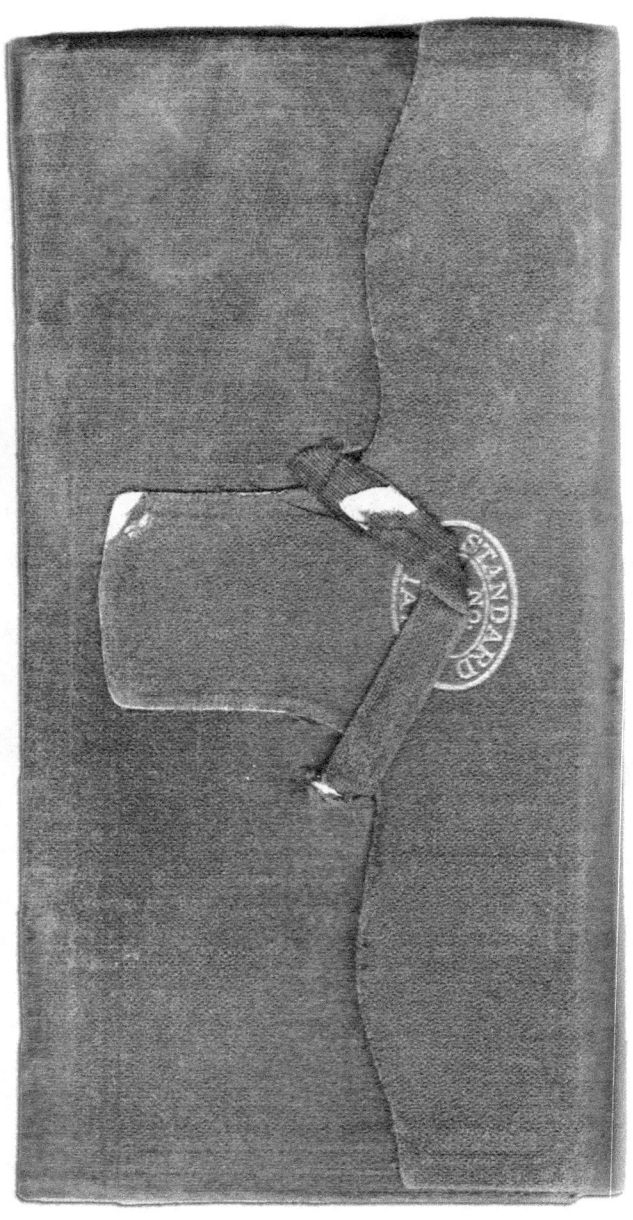

Emma's diary in its current condition.
Courtesy of the Eleanor Barnes Library, Elmira, New York.

Elmira is about 6 miles north of the Pennslyvania border in south central New York.

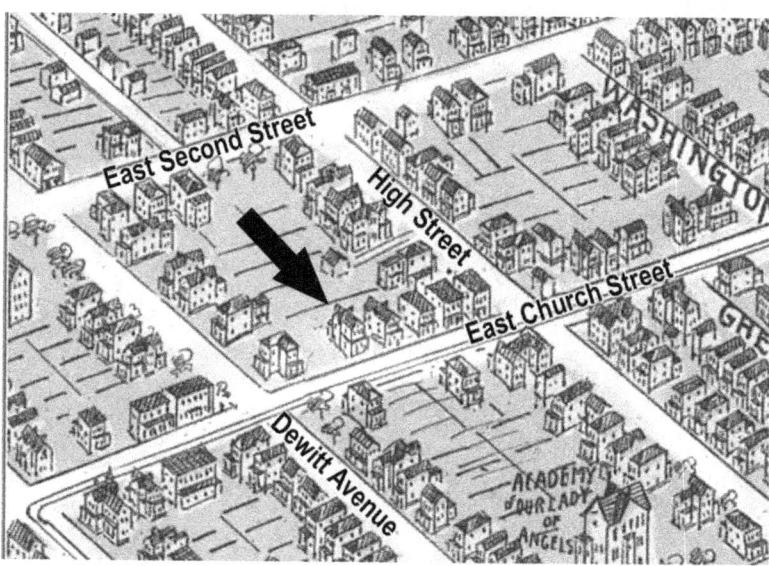

In 1902 Emma and Floyd Latier rented part of a house at 551 East Church Street. While in Elmira they moved around quite frequently. Almost every directory has them listed at a different address. This image is from the 1901 city map of Elmira (Library of Congress).

An image that was in the back pocket of Emma's diary.

Mrs. Emma Latier
Elmira, New York
1902

Wednesday, January 1, 1902
Floyd went to office as usual. Came home at 12:30 dinner. We took the [street] car to Calvin McKinney's. Staid to tea. We had a Happy New Year. So much to be thankful for. John [Emma's brother] came to 3:40 train this PM.

Thursday, January 2, 1902
Floyd went to office as usual. He came home with the good news of a hundred dollars advance on his salary. We are so pleased. John and I took [street] car to Arch Campbell's. Called to Cora Paul's & Mrs. Nichols's. Floyd went to Lodge. John & I been to Ella Taylor's.

Friday, January 3, 1902
Floyd went to office as usual. I am on [the] sick list at 9 A.M. We did not go out of doors all day. Lelia Brown and friend from P[Penn] Yan called tonight. John & I visited all day. Lottie W. called.

Saturday, January 4, 1902
Floyd went to office as usual. John and I visited all day. He and Floyd went up street tonight. I have a cold. Aunt Lydia staid to tea & evening.

Sunday, January 5, 1902
We did not go out today. John went out a while this P.M. Lottie Webster came here to dinner. Had a nice time all day. Cora & Clinton called. Just long enough to leave. Aunt Lydia packed.

Monday, January 6, 1902
Floyd went to office as usual. John went by the 10 A.M. train. We walked to P.O. for exercise. We both have colds. I worked about an hour on B.B. piece.

Sat. Jan. 4, 1902

Floyd went to Office as usual.
John and I visited all day. He and Floyd went up St. to night. I have a cold.
Aunt Lydia staid to tea & Evening.

Sunday 5

We did not go out to day. John went out a while this P.M. Lottie Webster came here to dinner. Had a nice time all day. Geo. & Clinton called just long enough to leave

Monday 6

Floyd went to Office as usual.
John went on the 10 A.M. train.
We walked to P.O. for exercise. We both have colds. I ironed about an hour on B.B. piece

Tues. Jan. 7, 1902

Floyd went to Office as usual.
I called to Mrs Palmer. She was not home. To Mrs Strattons & Mrs Stowells. We spent a lovely Evening at Mr & Mrs J. Johnsons.

Wednesday 8

Floyd went to Office as usual. He has a sore throat. Did not go out this Evening. Lottie called this P.M. It snows hard — fine sleighing

Thursday 9

Floyd went to Office as usual.
Aunt Lydia came to dinner. We went up St. this P.M.
Floyd went to Lodge tonight
Carrie S. called this P.M.

Tuesday, January 7, 1902
Floyd went to office as usual. I called to Mrs. Paltrowitz – she was not home – to Mrs. Stratton's and to Mrs. Stowell's. We spent a lovely evening at Mr. & Mrs. J. Johnson's.

Wednesday, January 8, 1902
Floyd went to office as usual. He had a sore throat. Did not go out this evening. Lottie called this P.M. It snows hard. Fine sleighing.

Thursday, January 9, 1902
Floyd went to office as usual. Aunt Lydia came to dinner. We went upstreet this P.M. Floyd went to Lodge tonight. Carrie S called this P.M.

Friday, January 10, 1902
Floyd went to office as usual. I worked on B.B. piece. Went downstreet after some se----. Mrs. Ganutz spent the evening here. The boys went to lodge. They gave Floyd a chance.

Saturday, January 11, 1902
Floyd went to office as usual. I worked on B.B. piece. Mrs. Nichols was here to dinner. Went about 3 PM. Floyd and I went downstreet tonight. I got a collar.

Sunday, January 12, 1902
We went to B. [Baptist?] Church in AM. To Miss Covill's in PM. Walked both ways. Cracked nuts and read & wrote this evening.

Monday, January 13, 1902
Floyd went to office as usual. I worked at BBP in the AM. Called to Mrs. C. Smith's & Mrs. VanWort's. Mrs. Riggs and daughter called this PM. We spent the evening at Mr. Johnson's.

Tuesday, January 14, 1902
Floyd went to office as usual. I worked at BBP in AM. Went to A. Campbell's. We came to Cora Paul's – went to Mr. Johnson's then to Mr. [George] Waters's art gallery [313 East Water Street].

Wednesday, January 15, 1902
Floyd went to office as usual. I called to Mrs. Mathews's then went upstreet for her. Ella & George came over this evening.

Thursday, January 16, 1902
Floyd went to office as usual. I staid in all day and read *Journal* [*Ladies' Home Journal*] this PM. Floyd went to lodge.

Friday, January 17, 1902
Floyd went to office as usual. I swept the hall and cleaned up kitchen this AM. Mrs. Nichols came to dinner. She and I took car [streetcar]. I went to Cora's. Mr. P [Paul] bought me home.

Saturday, January 18, 1902
Mr. Mathews is sick in bed. Floyd went to office as usual. I went down street this AM. Bought 4¾ yards of silk like my foulard [a type of fabric]. Mrs. Paltrowitz called this PM. We did not go out this evening.

Sunday, January 19, 1902
We went to church both morning and evening. Walked out a few minutes in PM to PO [Post Office] and went to a fire on John Street & wrote letters. No one came.

Monday, January 20, 1902
Floyd went to office as usual. I went up street for Mrs. Mathews. I called on her this PM. Cleaned the parlor in AM. Mr. Stowell & Lizzie was in this evening. Floyd paid her.

Tuesday, January 21, 1902
Floyd went to office as usual. Ella & I went downstreet this PM. I got rugs for BB. Worked a little on it this AM. We read this evening.

Wednesday, January 22, 1902
Floyd went to office as usual. It is terrible icy & wet slick. I worked on BB piece. We did not go out this evening, but read [instead].

Thursday, January 23, 1902
Floyd went to office as usual. I worked on BB piece all day as I could. Esther called. Floyd went to Lodge this evening.

Friday, January 24, 1902
Floyd went to office as usual. I ironed a few articles in AM. Called in PM to Mrs. Riggs's, Mrs. Roby's, Mr. Lewis's, Mrs. Stratton's & this evening we went to Mrs. Katzman's – had such a pleasant time.

Saturday, January 25, 1902
Floyd went to office as usual. I swept the 2 bedrooms good & cleaned the kitchen in PM. Took a [street] car up to Cora's. Floyd came up after office. We walked back. Called to Mrs. N. Did not go out.

Sunday, January 26, 1902
We staid at home all day. Read & wrote letters. Took them to PO at night. No one came. We do take such a lot of comfort together.

Monday, January 27, 1902
Floyd went to office as usual. I am on sick list at 10AM. Did not go out this evening.

Tuesday, January 28, 1902
Floyd went to office as usual. I worked on BB all day. We went over to Ella's this evening. Played cards.

Wednesday, January 29, 1902
Floyd went to office as usual. I did up ironing. Lottie came to dinner. I went downstreet – got more rugs for BB. We did not go out this evening.

Thursday, January 30, 1902
Floyd went to office as usual. I went down to Mrs. Mathews's this AM a few minutes. Mr. Paul came down. I went home with him. Walked back. Floyd went to Lodge. I was over to Ella's – played cards.

Friday, January 31, 1902
Floyd went to office as usual. Lottie's desk went this AM. I put everything away. Worked on BB piece, We went to Mrs. Mathews's for awhile this evening.

Saturday, February 1, 1902
Floyd went to office as usual. Ella & I went downstreet this AM. I got goods for waist. Esther came this PM also Lottie staid to tea. Esther came back for the evening.

Sunday, February 2, 1902
We did not go out today. Read, wrote letters. Read the *Journal.* It has been a wet sleet day. No one has been in.

Monday, February 3, 1902
Floyd went to office as usual. I went up to office this AM. Saw Mrs. S. Called to Esther's. Went downstreet. It's very cold this evening. We went up to Bill's for the evening.

Tuesday, February 4, 1902
Floyd went to office as usual. I worked all day on BB piece at intervals. Ella came up awhile. Will Covill was here to dinner. Lizzie came up tonight. Mr. & Mrs. Slater spent the evening.

Wednesday, February 5, 1902
Floyd went to office as usual. I finished the grape BB piece. Went up street. Bought oilcloth & a stand. Cleaned the bathroom this PM. Floyd nearly put down oilcloth but Ella & George came for the evening.

Thursday, February 6, 1902
Floyd went to office as usual. I cleaned all the morning – hall and dining room. Esther, Mr. & Mrs. Mathews, I invited to tea & spend the evening. Mr. M & Floyd went to Lodge. We played poker.

Friday, February 7, 1902
Floyd went to office as usual. I went upstreet with Esther at 10AM. She

Mon. Feb. 3, 1902

Floyd went to Office as usual. I went up to Office this a.m. Saw Mrs — called to Esther's. Went down St. It's very cold this eve. M— went up to Bell for the evening.

Tuesday 4

Floyd went to Office as usual. I worked all day on BB piece at intervals. Ella came up awhile. Mrs. Will Corll was here to dinner. Lizzie came up. Tonight Mr & Mrs Slater spent the evening.

Wednesday 5

Floyd went to Office as usual. I finished the Grape BB piece. Went up St. Bought oil cloth & a stand. Cleaned the Bath room this P.M. Floyd nearly put down oil cloth but Ella

Thurs. Feb. 6, 1902

Floyd went to Office as usual. I cleaned all the morning. Hall & dining room. Esther, Mr & Mrs Mather I invited to tea & spend the evening. Mr M— & Floyd went to Lodge. We played poker.

Friday 7

Floyd went to Office as usual. I went up St. with Esther at 9 a.m. She had all of her teeth out. I called to Mrs Mess— and dress makers this P.M. Did not go out this eve have a headache.

Saturday 8

Floyd went to Office as usual. I went up St. this a.m. payed for stand & oil cloth. We played poker by ourselves this eve. I ironed this P.M.

LYCEUM THEATER.

James O'Neill in "Monte Cristo" this evening.

"From the Farm to the White House" Friday evening.

"Cross Road of Life" Saturday evening.

"San Toy" Monday evening Feb. 17.

Chauncey Olcott in "Garrett O'Magh," Friday and Saturday February 21 and 22.

"Monte Cristo."

At the Lyceum to-night James O'Neill and a notable supporting company will be seen in Liebler & Co.'s great scenic production of Monte Cristo, which ran all last season in New York, Boston and Chicago. Mr. O'Neill is recognized as being the leading romantic actor on the English speaking stage. He endows the leading role of Edmond Dantes with a virility and romantic force that are remarkable. The production of Monte Cristo is said to be the most elaborate affair from a scenic standpoint that has ever been seen on our stage.

From the evening edition of the *Elmira Daily Gazette*, February 13, 1902.

had all of her teeth out. I called up to Mrs. Messinger's and dressmakers this PM. Did not go out this evening. Have a headache.

Saturday, February 8, 1902
Floyd went to office as usual. I went upstreet this AM. Paid for stand & oil cloth. We played poker by ourselves this evening. I ironed this PM.

Sunday, February 9, 1902
We went to the Baldwin Street Presbyterian church this AM. We read, wrote letters. Visited by ourselves. No one called.

Monday, February 10, 1902
Floyd went to office as usual. I went downstreet this PM. Got ribbon, hchiefs [handkerchiefs], etc. Lillian K came after we returned home. We went to Esther's this evening.

Tuesday, February 11, 1902
Floyd went to office as usual. I went downstreet this AM. Went over to Mrs. Brown this PM. I started to work the pink & green pillow. We spent the evening at George's playing cards.

Wednesday, February 12, 1902
Floyd went to office as usual. I went downstreet this AM. In PM sewed pieces in my suit jacket under the ---& went over to Mrs. Brown's did not go out this evening.

Thursday, February 13, 1902
Floyd went to office as usual. Mrs. B finished the white waist today. I wore it to Dr. Noble's sister's thimble party. Afterward we all went to the theatre. Floyd went to Lodge. We heard "Monte Cristo" played by James O'Neal.

Friday, February 14, 1902
Floyd went to office as usual. I was over to Mrs. B this AM. Went to Esther's – spent the PM. Mrs. B., Lelia & Fanny came over tonight. Floyd went to Lodge.

Saturday, February 15, 1902
Floyd went to office as usual. I cleaned up this AM. Lillian K came down. We went out looking at houses. Frank Ashcraft came & staid all night.

Sunday, February 16, 1902
Floyd & Frank went up to office to look around. He went of 5:20 train. Floyd went to Depot with him. This evening we went to Mr. Waters's, the artist. Brought home the picture.

Monday, February 17, 1902
Floyd went to office as usual. I worked on pillow pink & green squares on screen. Lelia, Mrs. Ina called. Esther was here to tea. Bill & Mr. Webber came. We all played cards.

Tuesday, February 18, 1902
Floyd went to office as usual. Floyd took his first lesson in physical culture. Mrs. Slater called.

Wednesday, February 19, 1902
Floyd went to office as usual. I cleaned, made a berry pie, washed the inside of the hall windows, etc. Walked up to Mr. Farris's – was not home. Stopped to Bill's.

Thursday, February 20, 1902
Floyd went to office as usual. I worked all day on the pillows. Mrs. Mathews & Mrs. Jones called. Floyd went to Lodge tonight.

Friday, February 21, 1902
On sick list 7:30AM. Floyd went to office as usual. I worked on sofa pillows. Did not go out this evening.

Saturday, February 22, 1902
Floyd went to office as usual. Did not go up this PM because of ½ holiday. I called to Mrs. Noble's & Mrs. Mathews's. Did not go out this evening.

Sunday, February 23, 1902
We attended Baptist Church this AM. Walked to Lillian's toward night. They were not at home. We had a nice time all day. Mrs. & Mrs. Mathews called.

Monday, February 24, 1902
Floyd went to office as usual. I went to Esther's & Mrs. Paltrowitz's this AM calling. This PM Lillian came down. We went to look at the house on Dewitt Street.

Tuesday, February 25, 1902
Floyd went to office as usual. I ironed in AM. Read the *Ladies Home Journal* in PM. In evening Lelia, Mrs. Heller, and Mrs. Clark Smith called. Did not go out this evening.

Wednesday, February 26, 1902
Floyd went to office as usual. I went to matinee called "The Counterfeiter's Daughter" with Mrs. Mathews & company. Went to Laskaris's for cream [ice cream]. Did not go out tonight.

Thursday, February 27, 1902
Floyd went to office as usual. Went upstreet in AM looking for a skirt. Was over to Mrs. Brown's this PM calling. Floyd went to Lodge.

Friday, February 28, 1902
Floyd went to office as usual. He went to Lodge tonight. I went downstreet this AM – bought a lot of things. Went to the Madison Avenue bridge. The river is raging.

Saturday, March 1, 1902
At 6:30AM the diking broke over at Madison Avenue. The greatest flood Elmira has witnessed. We watched it all day – 23 inches on the sidewalk – cellar full. Ella & George came tonight.

Sunday, March 2, 1902
The flood is slowly going down. Rained nearly all day. Mr. Mathews came for Floyd's boots. He went out sightseeing. We have heat – lots to eat.

Monday, March 3, 1902
Floyd went to office as usual. The water has gone down around the house. We went upstreet this evening. I was up in PM.

Tuesday, March 4, 1902
Floyd went to office as usual. The water has about all gone except cellars. I ripped up Mrs. J's black skirt. Floyd went to Lodge.

Wednesday, March 5, 1902
Floyd went to office as usual. I went upstreet this AM with Mrs. J. Attended the china sale. I got 4 plates. We did not go out this evening.

Thursday, March 6, 1902
Floyd went to office as usual. I called to Mrs. Cole's, Mrs. Paltrowitz's & Esther in AM. We went downstreet this PM. He went to lodge tonight.

Friday, March 7, 1902
Floyd went to office as usual. I worked some on pillow. We went up to Mr. Farr's speech this evening. Playing cards.

Saturday, March 8, 1902
Floyd went to office as usual. I went over the [Chemung] river [to the Southside] with Mrs. Taylor & picked out my paper. Floyd & I went downstreet tonight.

Sunday, March 9, 1902
We stayed home this AM. Rained some. Florence Riggs, Mrs. Webber & Esther came this PM. Tonight we walked up to Cora's.

Monday, March 10, 1902
Floyd went to office as usual. I cleaned the kitchen. The paperhanger came. It looks fine. We went to the Lyceum [theatre] tonight [to a show] called "Man of Mystery."

Tuesday, March 11, 1902
Floyd went to office as usual. I am on sick list. Did not go out today. Esther called & Mrs. Riggs.

A view down Carroll Street looking east during the 1902 flood. The Lyceum Theater was on the corner of Carroll and Lake Streets just behind the photographer.

LYCEUM THEATER.

Murray and Mack stock company in "A Man of Mystery" this evening.

"Florodora" Tuesday evening.

"Bonnie Brier Bush" Thursday evening.

"A Man of Mystery."

The Murray and Mackey Bon Ton Ideals open their week's engagement at the Lyceum this evening with a four-act comedy drama by Mark E. Swan, entitled "A Man of Mystery," a piece which has won Mr. Swan applause in the front rank of dramatic literatures. The leading role of this piece will be in the hands of Elmira's favorite, J. M. Donivan, who is supported by some of the best people in repertoire.

From the *Elmira Daily Gazette*, March 10, 1902.

Emma Latier

Ther.   TUES. MAR. 11, 1902   Wea.

Floyd went to Office as usual. I am on sick list, did not go out to day. Esther called & Mr. Riggs

Ther.   WEDNESDAY 12   Wea.

Floyd went to Office as usual. I ironed in A.M. did not feel like doing any thing this P.M. dad not W.M.

Ther.   THURSDAY 13   Wea.

Floyd went to Office as usual. Went down St. this A.M. got curtains for Bedroom took ones back this P.M.

Ther.   FRI. MAR. 14, 1902   Wea.

Floyd went to Office as usual. I swept the dining room, dressed to go to the church supper — did not feel one bit well. Ella staid with me.

Ther.   SATURDAY 15   Wea.

Floyd went to Office as usual. I washed doilies. Esther & I went down St. this P.M. Floyd & I went to Dr. Noble he gave me medicine.

Ther.   SUNDAY 16   Wea.

We did not go out to day. Had a quiet pleasant Sunday. My cough is quite bad. Lela brought over some horse radish.

Wednesday, March 12, 1902
Floyd went to office as usual. I ironed in AM. Did not feel like doing anything this PM, so did not. We were alone this evening. Had a nice time.

Thursday, March 13, 1902
Floyd went to office as usual. Went downstreet this AM – got curtains for bedroom. Took --- back this PM.

Friday, March 14, 1902
Floyd went to office as usual. I swept the dining room. Dressed to go to church supper. Did not feel one bit well. Ella staid with me. The boys went to Lodge.

Saturday, March 15, 1902
Floyd went to office as usual. I washed doilies. Esther & I went downstreet this PM. Floyd & I went to Dr. Noble. He gave me medicine.

Sunday, March 16, 1902
We did not go out today. Had a quiet pleasant Sunday. My cough is quite bad. Lelia brought over some horseradish.

Monday, March 17, 1902
Floyd went to office as usual. I went down to Mrs. Mathews's. She was not home. We went over to George's. Spent to the evening playing cards.

Tuesday, March 18, 1902
Floyd went to office as usual. I went over to Mrs. Brown's & to Mrs. Messinger's & Ella calling. Mr. & Mrs. Mathews was here this evening.

Wednesday, March 19, 1902
Floyd went to office as usual. I ironed in AM. Made a cherry & berry pie. Did my mending this morning.

L. L. Laskaris had an ice cream and candy parlor at 131 East Water Street in Elmira. "His candies and ice cream are the best ever." Postcard shows Laskaris store. Published by The Valentine & Sons Co., New York.

Image below from the *Elmira Daily Gazette*, November 18, 1904.

BIG DISPLAY OF FINE CANDY
FOR THIS WEEK AND SATURDAY

Our prices will surprise you. Our Chewing Candy is selling fast. Nut Caramels a specialty. Don't forget Laskaris' famous Ice Cream Soda and our delicious Hot Chocolate with whipped cream.

LASKARIS

Thursday, March 20, 1902
Floyd went to office as usual. Esther & I went downstreet this PM. We spent the evening at Webber's. Played cards.

Friday, March 21, 1902
Floyd went to office as usual. Mrs. Paltrowitz, Lizzie, & Grace called. I was over to Mrs. I--- a few moments. Ella & I went downstreet. We were in this evening.

Saturday, March 22, 1902
Floyd went to office as usual. I went downstreet this AM. Ordered a black silk skirt. Lula Dale was in this Evening. Floyd went to special lodge meeting.

Sunday, March 23, 1902
Mr. & Mrs. Paltrowitz were here to dinner "invited." I am on sick list – not time. Esther. Louise Geiger & Mildred Shaw called this PM.

Monday, March 24, 1902
Floyd went to office as usual. I went downstreet this PM. Tried on my skirt. Mr. Shoemaker called between 3 & 4 had a nice visit. We spent the evening at Joe Bryan's.

Tuesday, March 25, 1902
Floyd went to office as usual. I just worked as little as possible - layed down in PM. This evening we went to call to Mr. Emblem's then went to Dr. Henry's reception. Then to Laskaris's.

Wednesday, March 26, 1902
Floyd went to office as usual. He took 1st degree in the Chapter tonight. Ella & I went downstreet and to church this PM. I finished filling my screen.

Thursday, March 27, 1902
Floyd went to office as usual. I called to Mrs. Mathews's & Mrs. Messinger's. We went to Esther's reception for Louise Geiger. Lizzie, Florence Riggs, Ray Shoemaker called.

Friday, March 28, 1902

Floyd went to office as usual. Mrs. Messinger called this PM. George & Floyd went to Lodge. Ella & I staid up until 11PM.

Saturday, March 29, 1902

Floyd went to office as usual. I made a lemon pie and a cake this PM. We went downstreet this evening.

Sunday, March 30, 1902

We went to Easter services at Baptist Church. Read in PM. Clinton & Cora came – staid to lunch. Then we all went to Masonic services.

Monday, March 31, 1902

Floyd went to office as usual. I went over to Lizzie's this PM. We played on zither tonight – had a nice time by ourselves.

Tuesday, April 1, 1902

Floyd went to office as usual. I did my ironing. Went upstreet paid insurance (Casualty). Picked my picture frames for fruit pieces. Then I called to Esther's. George & Ella came.

Wednesday, April 2, 1902

Floyd went to office as usual. We walked out this evening. Bought some bananas.

Thursday, April 3, 1902

I have a lovely birthday. Floyd went to office in PM. In PM he joined the Masonic Parade to the corner stone laying of the Federal [Post office at the corner of Church and State Streets]. I went with Ella. Mr. & Mrs. Webber, Mr. & Mrs. Cole came tonight. Floyd went to Lodge.

Friday, April 4, 1902

Floyd went to office as usual. I finished the pink & green "square" pillow. Mrs. Ina, Lizzie & Grace came in tonight. We read alone.

"In the corner stone is a receptacle in which will be place in a copper box.... The copper case will be filled with records and placed in the corner stone to be sealed up for probably a hundred years. The copper case will contain the local roster of all Masonic bodies, program of exercises, copies of Elmira newspapers, list of federal officials connected with the erection of the building, Tribune almanac, World almanac, court calendar, orgnization of city government, organization of state government, organization of the grand lodge of F. &A.M. of New York State, organization of Elmira schools, organization of Elmira Free Academy, organization of Elmira College, list of invited federal officials. The box is just the size of four bricks."

Elmira Daily Gazette and Free Press, April 2, 1902

LAYING CORNER STONE OF FEDERAL BUILDING

Program of the Masonic Ceremonies To-Morrow.

FINAL DETAILS CONCLUDED TO-DAY

Masonic Bodies of City Will Meet at the Temple and, Headed by Mulcare's Band, March To the Scene of Exercises—General Public Invited.

Elmira's post office on East Church Street. The lobby had Vermont marble walls, oak woodwork, and a beautiful marble staircase. The building still exists although not as a post office. Publisher: Paul C. Koeber Company, NY.

Saturday, April 5, 1902
Floyd went to office as usual. I went downtown. Paid Mr. Read [G.W.H. Read, Old City Hall Art Gallery] for frames. We did not go out tonight.

Sunday, April 6, 1902
We went to church this PM. It rained this PM and evening. No one came in. We had a good time by ourselves.

Monday, April 7, 1902
Floyd went to office as usual. I cut out ruffle for pillow (pink). We spent the evening over to George's.

Tuesday, April 8, 1902
Floyd went to office as usual. I ironed in AM. Went over to Lizzie this PM. We made the pink pillows. We did not go out this evening. It rains.

Wednesday, April 9, 1902
Floyd went to office as usual. I cleaned a little in the clothes room. Washed bottles. Cleaned the medicine case. Floyd went to Lodge. It rained all day.

Thursday, April 10, 1902
Floyd went to office as usual. I called to Mrs. P, Mrs. B & Stowell. I worked on shell doily. Floyd went to lodge tonight. Lizzie & Grace came in the afternoon to tea.

Friday, April 11, 1902
Floyd went to office as usual. I went downstreet this AM. Bought a hat, shirtwaist goods for Lottie Webster, a waist and ties. Floyd went to lodge tonight.

Saturday, April 12, 1902
Floyd went to office this AM. This PM we left on Lehigh [train] for Cortland – arrived there at 6. It rained tonight. We sat up late.

Sunday, April 13, 1902
We visited all day. It was a dark cold day. Tonight we 4 attended the Congregational Church – heard Rev. Fuller of Corning.

Monday, April 14, 1902
We came home by way of Binghamton – arrived here at 1 PM. Got a lunch. Then the Standard [Standard Oil Company] all attended Mr. Howland's funeral as a body.

Tuesday, April 15, 1902
Floyd went to office as usual. I did my ironing. Went over to Mrs. Brown's this PM.

Wednesday, April 16, 1902
Floyd went to office as usual. I went over to Mrs. Stowell's this PM a little while.

Thursday, April 17, 1902
Floyd went to office as usual. Ella & I went downstreet this PM. Floyd went to lodge. I put binding on my bicycle skirt.

Friday, April 18, 1902
Floyd went to office as usual. Ella, her mother, Esther & I went up to Esther's this PM. I went up to Esther's this AM on wheel [bicycle]. Floyd & I went out riding [bicycles] for the first time. George & Ella came here tonight.

Saturday, April 19, 1902
Floyd went to office as usual. We went to over to George after 4 until supper time. They were over this evening.

Sunday, April 20, 1902
We went to church this AM. This PM we walked to Mrs. Nichols's & to Cora's. They were not home. Spent a nice evening by ourselves.

Monday, April 21, 1902
Floyd went to office as usual. I went downstreet this PM. Bought a duck skirt. George & Ella – we all sat on porch this evening.

Tuesday, April 22, 1902
Floyd went to office as usual. I was over to Mrs. Brown's & to Ella's this afternoon. We went down to Mr. Berner's – got groceries.

Fresh Mushrooms
Hot House Tomatoes and Cucumbers.
F. A. BERNER
501-603 E. Water St.

From the *Elmira Daily Gazette*, November 28, 1906.

Lyceum Theatre
SATURDAY EVENING, APRIL 26.
First Time Here of the Big Comedy Success.

ARIZONA

Produced on a Grand Scale By
LA SHELLE AND HAMLIN'S
COMPLETE METROPOLITAN
COMPANY.

A production of note. Identically the same as in all large cities. "Arizona" the play that pleases all. Comedy—Heart Interest—Pathos. Prices not raised. $1.00, 75c 50c, and 25c. Secure seats early at Box Office. Seats on sale Thursday, April 24.

Lyceum Theatre
One Week, Opening Monday, April 28.
Night Prices, 10c, 20c, 30c and 50c.
Matinee Every Day Starting Tuesday—10c—
No Higher.

WILBUR OPERA CO.

And great vaudeville bill including Baby Mascotte Corinne and a bunch of white faced pickaninnies; the Gardner children; coon songs and cake walks; illustrated songs that make the feet tap, Amazon marches.
Note—Ladies admitted free Monday night if accompanied by a gentleman with paid 30 or 50 cent ticket. Prices, 10, 20, 30 and 50c.
Special Souvenir Matinee Thursday.
First 500 ladies attending to receive ¼ pound of Chocolate Bon Bons.
Seats on sale Friday, April 25th.

From the *Elmira Daily Gazette*, April 26, 1902.

Wednesday, April 23, 1902
Floyd went to office as usual. Mrs. Brown came over and made my Lobster Salad. Dr. N & sister were here to supper. She was not well, but had a nice time.

Thursday, April 24, 1902
Floyd went to office as usual. I called to Mrs. T----'s & Mrs. VanNort's this PM. Went to George's this evening. Played cards.

Friday, April 25, 1902
Floyd went to office as usual. I mopped, did a general cleaning up. Floyd went to lodge, then came to Esther's. She had an evening's visit. Mrs. Nichols spent the PM here.

Saturday, April 26, 1902
Floyd went to office as usual. Mother L [Latier/Litteer] came on 3:40 train N.C. [Northern Central] We met her. We went to the Lyceum Theatre – play "Arizona."

Sunday, April 27, 1902
We staid in all day. Mother has sick headache in AM.

Monday, April 28, 1902
Floyd went to office as usual. Mother & I went downstreet in AM & PM. We went to Lyceum [opera] tonight.

Tuesday, April 29, 1902
Floyd went to office as usual. I ironed in AM. Lizzie & Mrs. T came. George & Ella called tonight. Floyd went to lodge.

Wednesday, April 30, 1902
Floyd went to office as usual. Mother & I went downstreet this PM [afternoon?]and called to Mrs. VanNort's. Did not go out this PM [evening?].

Thursday, May 1, 1902
Floyd went to office as usual. We went downstreet today AM. Mrs. Dale and Ella called. We all went to Mr. Shoemaker's to tea.

Ther.   TUES. APRIL 22, 1902   Wea.

Floyd went to Office as usual. I was over to Mrs Brown's & to Ella's this afternoon. We went down to Mr Berner's, got groceries.

Ther.   WEDNESDAY 23   Wea.

Floyd went to Office as usual. Mrs Brown came over and made my Potato Salad. Dr N & sister were here to supper, she was not well but had a nice time.

Ther.   THURSDAY 24   Wea.

Floyd went to office as usual. I called to Mrs Simpson's & Mrs Van- Nor to this P.M. went to George's this eve. Played cards.

Ther.   FRI. APRIL 25, 1902   Wea.

Floyd went to Office as usual. I mopped, did a general cleaning up. Floyd went to lodge, then came to Esther's, she had an evening visit. Eva and Michael spent the P.M. here.

Ther.   SATURDAY 26   Wea.

Floyd went to Office as usual. Mother L. came on 3.40 train N.C. We met her, then we went to the Lyceum, played Arizona.

Ther.   SUNDAY 27   Wea.

We staid in all day. Mother has sick head-ache in a.m.

Above: The Northern Central Railroad used the Erie Depot in Elmira. Publisher: Leighton & Valentine, NYC. Below: the Madison Avenue bridge. Publisher: unknown.

Emma Latier

The interior of the Lyceum Theater on Lake Street. Photograph courtesy of the Eleanor Barnes Library, Elmira, New York.

Opposite, above: West Water Street looking west. Publisher: Paul C. Koeber, New York City. Below: East Water Street looking west. Publisher: unknown.

6532 Elmira N. Y. West Water Street.

7684—East Water St., looking West, Elmira, N. Y.

Trinity Episcopal Church on Main Street. Publisher: unknown.

Above: The Sly home on the corner of Sly Street and Maple Avenue. Publisher: Miss Jeanette Adams, Elmira. Below: William Street looking north. Publisher unknown.

A 8813 Water Street, Elmira, N.Y.

May 31 1906
Dear Edith how are you & tell you a letter would be a great pleasure to me as been a long time since I have heard from you Love to all and Lizzie

Elmira College's observatory at the corner of Sixth Street and Park Place was built in 1858 and razed in 1939.

Opposite, above East Water Street looking east - on the left is the Rathbun Hotel. Publisher: The Rotograph Company, New York. Below is Lake Street area of the courthouse complex. Publisher: Souvenir Post Card Company, New York.

Friday, May 2, 1902

Floyd went to office as usual. Mother & I went this AM to Cora's and Carrie Latier's also. Downstreet to the No. 8 [Lagonegro school] exercises this PM. Mame Noble called.

Saturday, May 3, 1902

Floyd went to office as usual. Mother went on 10 AM train. Mabelle P came at 10:30. We all went to the basketball game at YMCA. Then went downstreet.

Sunday, May 4, 1902

We went to Baptist church this AM. Ray took Mabel riding this PM. We spent the evening here. Mr. & Mrs J. Mathews, Mrs. June M called.

Monday, May 5, 1902

Floyd went to office as usual. I went downstreet with Mabel. She took car for Watkins [Glen]. George, Ella, Floyd & I went to the play "The Deacon's Daughter."

Tuesday, May 6, 1902

Floyd went to office as usual. I cleaned out dresser drawers & ironed. Started the gasoline stove today. Mrs. & Mrs. Emblem came down tonight.

Wednesday, May 7, 1902

Floyd went to office as usual. Mrs. T helped me clean 2 bedrooms & hall. I showed house tonight.

Thursday, May 8, 1902

Floyd went to office as usual. I went downstreet this PM and took hat from Rosenbaum's to Mrs. Winkle. We spent the evening at Dr. Noble's – had a nice time.

Friday, May 9, 1902

Floyd went to office as usual. I trained up the wild cucumbers some this PM. Ironed sash curtains in AM. Ella, Esther, & Mrs. L was up this evening. Floyd went to lodge.

Saturday, May 10, 1902
Floyd went to office as usual. George, Ella, Floyd & I went downstreet tonight. Picked out a chair for Mr. Ganutz's birthday. Floyd has got an awful cold.

Sunday, May 11, 1902
We went up to Cora Paul's this PM. Floyd's cold is very bad. Got home tonight at 10 PM.

Monday, May 12, 1902
Floyd went to office as usual. I called to 8 homes this PM. Ella & I went to the May Festival rehearsal at Hedding Church tonight. The boys went to Mr. Ganutz's surprise party.

Tuesday, May 13, 1902
Floyd went to office as usual. I went to Lyceum this AM to get reserved seats. Ella, Esther, Mrs. Messinger, & myself went to Matinee in PM. We did not go out this PM.

Wednesday, May 14, 1902
Floyd went to office as usual. His cold is bad. Went to Dr. N tonight. Mrs. J and I went to Matinee. Ella & I went wheel riding to her mother's. Ella & George came in a few minutes this evening.

Thursday, May 15, 1902
Floyd went to office as usual. I went over on wheel to see Mrs. Wilson & Katie Bruedich [Burdick?]. In PM Ella & I went to Lyceum matinee. Floyd & I went this evening to Lyceum – see the beautiful Mrs. Dorothy Harvey [opera singer].

Friday, May 16, 1902
Floyd went to office as usual. I swept & cleaned up in general this AM. Went to depot to meet Aunt Emma – came on 3:40 N.C. [Northern Central]. We 3 went to "Joan of Arc" at Lyceum tonight.

Saturday, May 17, 1902
Floyd went to office as usual. He went to the depot at 5AM to meet

Uncle Dan. Aunt Emma & Uncle D spent the day at Mr. Stowell's[?] Then went on 5:20 train for Hornell. Cora & Clinton was here to supper. George & Ella spent the evening with us.

Sunday, May 18, 1902
Did not get up until 11:30 AM. Did not go anywhere today. Mr. & Mrs. Messinger, Mr. & Mrs. Cramer, Mr. & Mrs. Rebben[?], George Taylor, Mr. & Mrs. Stowell & Lizzie called this PM.

Monday, May 19, 1902
Floyd went to office as usual. I didn't do anything all day. We went over to George & Ella's tonight.

Tuesday, May 20, 1902
Floyd went to office as usual. I ironed this AM, went downstreet this PM, cleaned my white waist with gasoline. George & Ella, Mr. & Mrs. Cramer, we played cards this evening.

Wednesday, May 21, 1902
Floyd went to office as usual. Was over to Lizzie's this PM. Floyd took Royal Arch Degree in Mason's tonight.

Thursday, May 22, 1902
Floyd went to office as usual. I went downstreet this PM. Bought a lot of trinkets. We rode on wheels this evening. Then met Father L [Latier/Litteer] at 9:06 Erie RR.

Friday, May 23, 1902
Floyd went to office as usual. Father & I went to depot to meet Mama – she did not come.

Saturday, May 24, 1902
Floyd went to office as usual. Father & I went to "Brightest America" matinee. Father & Floyd went downstreet tonight. Esther & Lizzie called.

MAY MUSIC FESTIVAL IS PLEASANT MEMORY

From the *Elmira Daily Gazette*, May 17, 1902.

Week of Melody Concluded By the Concert at Lyceum Theater.

WAS MOST FITTING CLIMAX

Bridal Chorus From "Rose Maiden" and the Historic Cantata "Joan of Arc" Were Sung — Soloists Won New Honors by Their Work.

"IN BRIGHTEST AMERICA."

Last Production of the Carnival to be Given at the Auditorium This Evening.

From the *Elmira Daily Gazette*, May 26, 1902.

"In Brightest America" the Business Men's carnival given under the auspices of the Alpha club was repeated at the Auditorium Saturday afternoon with the same success that marked the Friday night performance. The entertainment is worthy the best of patronage, setting aside the object of the club in producing it. There is a fine program this evening and it is expected that a large audience will witness it. The production has been well attended and a record breaking audience is expected this evening.

Sunday, May 25, 1902

Did not go out until this evening. Had an electric shower this PM. Went to Memorial services at Hedding church tonight.

Monday, May 26, 1902

Floyd went to office this AM – did not go back in PM but he & Father went to Rorick's [Glen] and Eldridge Park. Floyd went to Masonic banquet tonight.

Tuesday, May 27, 1902

Floyd went to office as usual – but came to the train to see Father away at 10 – N.C. [Northern Central]. This evening George & Ella, Floyd & me went to Elmira Heights for a Macabee entertainment.

Wednesday, May 28, 1902

Floyd went to office as usual. Ella & I went downstreet this AM. I bought a daisy hat and pink s[hirt] waist.

Thursday, May 29, 1902

Floyd went to office as usual. I was down to see Mrs. Mathews's. Floyd went to Lodge. Mrs. Emblem staid with me & we went to spiritual meeting.

Friday, May 30, 1902

We had an early dinner – took a car for Eldridge Park. Had a lovely day together. Ella & George came over. We played cards this evening.

Saturday, May 31, 1902

Floyd went to office as usual. I went upstreet after 4 PM. Paid several little bills. Ella staid here. The boys went upstreet this evening.

Sunday, June 1, 1902

I am on sick list this PM. Floyd and I went to Baptist Church. Sat on porch this PM.

Monday, June 2, 1902

Floyd went to office as usual. We commenced taking our meals with

Above: Eldridge Park. Publisher: The Valentine & Sons Publishing Co., New York.
Below: A glass negative print of beautiful Eldridge Park and casino circa 1895. Library of Congress, Prints and Photographs Division, Detroit Publishing Company Collection. LC-D4-12079

Rorick's Glen theatre. Publisher: C.S. Woolworth & Co., Elmira, NY.

Mrs. T [Taylor – owned the house where they lodged] at $5.50 a week. We spent the evening at Dr. Noble's.

Tuesday, June 3, 1902
Floyd went to office as usual, but commenced to come home at 12 in stead of 1:15PM. I ironed in AM. Sat on porch in PM. A thunder shower tonight.

Wednesday, June 4, 1902
Floyd went to office as usual. Mr. Paul came. We went downstreet – bought Cora lots of things. He staid to tea. George & Ella came over – spent the evening.

Thursday, June 5, 1902
Floyd went to office as usual. I called to Esther's & Mrs. Roby's. Went downstreet. We sat on porch this evening. Then went over to Dr. Messinger's for a while.

Friday, June 6, 1902
Floyd went to office as usual. I called to Esther's & Mrs. Roby's. Went downstreet. We sat on porch this evening then went to Dr. Messenger's for a while.

Saturday, June 7, 1902
Floyd went to office as usual. I went to sleep this PM. My arm hurts. George, Ella, Floyd & I went to Chinese Laundry on Lake Street [Lee Ham's laundry 663 Lake Street].

Sunday, June 8, 1902
Went to Baptist church in AM and evening both. We had a nice time all day.

Monday, June 9, 1902
Floyd went to office as usual. I went downstreet with Ella this PM. Floyd & I rode wheels to call on Lillian Katzmann.

Tuesday, June 10, 1902
Floyd went to office as usual. I did my little ironing. We went over to George's tonight. Played cards.

Wednesday, June 11, 1902
Floyd went to office as usual. He went to the Chapter banquet tonight. Came home at 12:30. I sat on porch and waited for him. Will & Lillian K came down tonight.

Thursday, June 12, 1902
Floyd went to office as usual. I went over to Mrs. Paltrowitz's this AM. We went downstreet this PM. Got Mother black lace for a dress. We rode our wheels to [the] park tonight.

Friday, June 13, 1902
Floyd went to office as usual. I went out – found a woman to do my washing. Floyd went to lodge. Ella & I staid together.

Saturday, June 14, 1902
Floyd went to office as usual. We went downstreet tonight – got us each a pair of low shoes. It rained. We came home in a [street] car.

Sunday, June 15, 1902
We attended the Children's Day exercises at the ME [Methodist Episcopal] church in AM. Then Mr. & Mrs. Cramer came over tonight. We had a nice time all day by ourselves.

Monday, June 16, 1902
Floyd went to office as usual. I went downstreet – changed my low shoes after dinner. We rode to Lillian Katzman's and Mr. Emblem's this PM.

Tuesday, June 17, 1902
Floyd went to office as usual. Mrs. Hancock & Mrs. Slater, Mrs. Messinger, Esther, Mr. Ganutz called this PM. Ella & George came over this evening.

Wednesday, June 18, 1902
Floyd went to office as usual. I sat on porch all day. Floyd went to lodge tonight.

Thursday, June 19, 1902
Floyd went to office as usual. I was over to Mrs. Messinger's this PM. Dr. [&] Mrs. M [Messinger] & we went to the Band concert at Mason Park.

Friday, June 20, 1902
Floyd went to office as usual. He took the Red Cross degree tonight. Knight Templar. Ella & I went downstreet this PM – had a lot of fun.

Saturday, June 21, 1902
Floyd went to office as usual. Tonight is our last meal with Mrs. Taylor. We went into [?] tonight – bought groceries.

Sunday, June 22, 1902
We went to Baptish church this AM. Commenced H.K. at our tables. Presbyterian [church] tonight – heard Mr. Warlich sing. We went to Woodlawn [cemetery] in car. Macabee memorial service.

Monday, June 23, 1902
Floyd went to office as usual. Ella & I went upstreet this PM. We just walked out around the block this evening.

Tuesday, June 24, 1902
Floyd went to office as usual. I did my ironing as usual. I mended this PM. We sat on porch over to Ella's tonight.

Wednesday, June 25, 1902
Floyd went to office as usual. I went to Depot to meet John – he came on 3:40 [train]. Floyd went up to Lodge. Ella & George came over – played cards.

Thursday, June 26, 1902
Floyd went to office as usual. John & I went down to see Supt. Maloney this AM. Mr. Paul called tonight.

Friday, June 27, 1902
Floyd went to office as usual. John & I rode our wheel this PM. I went downstreet for Aunt Emma. Floyd took Templar degree.

Above: A quiet afternoon at Eldridge Park. Publisher: The Valentine & Sons Publishing Co., New York. Below: Entrance to Watkins Glen State Park. Photograph courtesy of the Eleanor Barnes Library, Elmira, New York.

Saturday, June 28, 1902
Floyd went to office as usual. I am on sick list 7:30 AM. Esther called this evening. We sat on porch this PM. Wrote letters.

Sunday, June 29, 1902
It just rained terrible all day. Floyd went up to see Mr. Waller a little while tonight.

Monday, June 30, 1902
Floyd went to office as usual. I went upstreet – paid insurance and got my daisy hat. We staid in and read this evening.

Tuesday, July 1, 1902
Floyd went to office as usual. John went to Rorick's [Glen]. Esther & Mr. [William] Starbird called tonight. Floyd went up to lodge. I went over to Lizzie's.

Wednesday, July 2, 1902
Floyd went to office as usual. Esther & I went downstreet this PM. Then I went to Depot - Mama did not come. Floyd, John & I went to Eldridge [Park] on wheels tonight.

Thursday, July 3, 1902
Floyd went to office as usual. He is working very hard – finished footing ledger today. Floyd went to lodge. I went over to Lizzie's. Esther called.

Friday, July 4, 1902
George, Ella, Floyd & I went to Watkins [Glen] – ate our lunch at 12. Then went through Havana Glen – did not rain. Had a nice time. John staid here.

Saturday, July 5, 1902
Floyd went to office as usual. It rained all day – hard. Esther came down tonight. Floyd took boots back. He went with her home.

Sunday, July 6, 1902
It rained most all day. Oh so damaging – near a flood. We walked down to river tonight. Esther & Mr. Starbird.

Thurs. July 3, 1902

Floyd went to Office as usual. He is working very hard. Finished posting Ledger to day. Floyd went to Lodge. I went over to Sophies. Esther called.

Friday 4

George Ella Floyd & I went to Watkins ate our lunch at 12 then went through Havana glen — did not rain. had a nice time.

Saturday 5

Floyd went to Office as usual. It rained all day hard. Esther came down tonight, wage Floyd took Jack, he went with

Sun. July 6, 1902

It rained most all day. oh so damaging, near a flood. we walked down to river tonight. Esther & Mr Starbird.

Monday 7

Floyd went to Office as usual. John & I went on wheels to Cora's got some onions lettuce & radishes called to Mrs Nichols George & Ella was over tonight.

Tuesday 8

Floyd went to Office as usual. We got a large water melon tonight. Mr & Mrs Whitman Carrie S & Mrs Bodworth called.

Lake Street looking north from East Water Street. Publisher: Rubin Bros., Elmira, NY.

Monday, July 7, 1902

Floyd went to office as usual. John & I went on wheels to Cora's – got some onions, lettuce, & radishes. Called to Mrs. Nichols's. George & Ella was over tonight.

Tuesday, July 8, 1902

Floyd went to office as usual. We got a large watermelon tonight. Mr. & Mrs. Whitmore, Carrie S & Mrs. Bodworth called.

Wednesday, July 9, 1902

Floyd went to office at 7 this AM. He is working awful hard. Ray is on vacation. John & I went downstreet this AM. We made rootbeer. I went up to SO [Standard Oil] office this AM on wheel. We went to Eldridge Park.

Thursday, July 10, 1902

Floyd went to office as usual. Esther & Mrs. Weigan called this PM. Mr. Emblem came tonight. John went with us to the Spiritualist church. Floyd & Mr. E went to lodge.

Friday, July 11, 1902

Floyd went to office as usual. John & I made a batch of cookies & mince pie this AM. Floyd & I went to the band concert tonight.

Saturday, July 12, 1902

Floyd went to office as usual. I cleaned up the house this AM. John, Floyd and I went to Eldridge Park on our wheels.

Sunday, July 13, 1902

John, Floyd & I went to Baptist church this AM. Had a quiet day on the porch. So happy George & Ella called this evening.

Monday, July 14, 1902

Floyd went to office as usual. I sat on our porch all day. We went over to Mrs. Roby's this evening. George & Ella came over to our house about 10. We ate watermelon.

Tuesday, July 15, 1902

Floyd went to office as usual. I ironed this AM. Ella & I went downstreet this PM then we went together with the boys to Mrs. Searles's on Clinton Street this evening.

Wednesday, July 16, 1902

Floyd went to office as usual. He is very busy since Mr. Mathews is on vacation. Ella & I called to Mrs. Slater's, Hancock's, Mathews's, Dale's, and Murdough's [Murdock?].

Thursday, July 17, 1902

Floyd went to office as usual. Made a huckleberry pie. I went up to Esther's this PM. Was over to Ella's a little while this evening.

Friday, July 18, 1902

Floyd went to office as usual. I went downstreet this PM. Got goods for a waist. Got 2 teeth filled. We played cards tonight – John & I. Floyd read.

Saturday, July 19, 1902

Floyd went to office as usual. John went home this morning on 10AM train. I went to depot with him – then to Esther's and dressmaker.

Sunday, July 20, 1902

It rained most all day. We did not get up until 10:30. We read, wrote letters, walked down and looked at the river rising tonight. Went to John Mathews's a little while.

Monday, July 21, 1902

Floyd went to office as usual. I went to the dressmaker's – she was sick. So sat on the porch in PM alone.

Tuesday, July 22, 1902

Floyd went to office as usual. I ironed, canned 5 quarts of huckleberries – spilled one quart on the floor – make an awful mess and canned 5 quarts of blackcaps [black raspberries]. Floyd fixed my wheel.

CIRCUS DAY, BEST OF ALL THE SUMMER

Forepaugh & Sells Brothers Monster Show Attracts Thousands.

CROWDS SAW DELAYED PARADE

Afternoon Performance Behind Schedule Time but Being Given Before an Immense Audience—Diavolo the Great Feature of the Show.

From the afternoon edition *Elmira Daily Gazette*, July 29, 1902. This was the first day of the circus. Watching the circus parade from the train station was a big deal. The Lackawanna train was late due to heavy rain between Elmira and Ithaca, and the crowd waited two hours along Maple Avenue for the parade of animals, performers, and five bands. The highlight of the circus was Diavolo "in his famous cycle ride of looping the loop."

Wednesday, July 23, 1902
Floyd went to office as usual. I made sugar & ginger cookies this AM.

Thursday, July 24, 1902
Floyd went to office as usual. Ella & I went downstreet this PM. We stayed home this evening.

Friday, July 25, 1902
Floyd went to office as usual. I washed bedroom windows. Ella & I went downstreet and to depot. George & Floyd went to lodge. Frank Ashcraft was to supper with us.

Saturday, July 26, 1902
Floyd went to office as usual. Frank Ashcraft, wife and son came. We went to Rorick's [Glen] tonight – had a nice time.

Sunday, July 27, 1902
We got up at 9AM. Frank & Floyd went to Eldridge [Park] this AM. We went to depot at 4:13 with them. We are alone this evening.

Monday, July 28, 1902
Floyd went to office as usual. I went to dressmaker's this AM & PM both. Called to Esther's. We were invited over to George's tonight – had ice cream.

Tuesday, July 29, 1902
Floyd went to office as usual. I ironed this AM. Went with Mrs. I--- to the Forepaugh & Sells Brothers Circus tonight. Floyd & I went to the show – had a nice time. A fine day.

Wednesday, July 30, 1902
Floyd went to office as usual. I went downstreet – took the car. Spent the PM with Lillian K – and Floyd & I went up there for the evening.

Thursday, July 31, 1902
Floyd went to office as usual. I did not do anything – so warm today. We went over to call to Mrs. JMS tonight. Floyd fixed my wheel before supper.

Friday, August 1, 1902

Floyd went to office as usual. Esther came down this AM. Staid to dinner. Went away about 2 [PM]. I went to dressmaker's after that. We went to PO tonight.

Saturday, August 2, 1902

Floyd came home at 12:20. Office closes Saturday PM. We went to Eldridge [Park] on our wheels and tonight George, Ella & we went to see Dan Quinlan's parade.

Sunday, August 3, 1902

O! What a quite lovely day we have had. Read, wrote letters. Took them to Office tonight.

Monday, August 4, 1902

Floyd went to office as usual. I went to dressmaker's this PM. We sat on porch this evening.

Tuesday, August 5, 1902

Floyd went to office as usual. I ironed this AM. Canned 4 quarts red caps. Sat on porch this evening.

Wednesday, August 6, 1902

Floyd went to office as usual. We & George & Ella walked up to Cora's tonight. She was not there.

Thursday, August 7, 1902

Floyd went to office as usual. He fixed my tire tonight. I went downstreet this AM.

Friday, August 8, 1902

Floyd went to office as usual. I went up to town on wheel this AM. Got discounts at F.E.D. Called to Mrs. Mathews's & dressmaker's. Ella, Esther called tonight. Packed the trunks. Floyd went to lodge.

Saturday, August 9, 1902

Floyd worked until 11:30. We started on 1:40 PM train on Erie [train] for Grove Springs - the train killed a woman. Father met us on porch.

Sunday, August 10, 1902
We drove up home this PM. Found all of our people home having a nice time.

Monday, August 11, 1902
Floyd went hunting. We are having a nice time.

Tuesday, August 12, 1902
Floyd & I went to Penn Yan on the *Mary Bell* [steamer] – had a pleasant day.

Wednesday, August 13, 1902
We went up home on our wheels this AM. An old man came there about 11 PM. Did not sleep much tonight.

Thursday, August 14, 1902
Floyd went down home fishing – came up tonight. Mama & I took Ned. I went to Phoebe Bailey's, May Covert's, Satie Kiefer's – got home at 3 PM.

Friday, August 15, 1902
Am on sick list. Mama & I went to Penn Yan. I came on the boat to the Grove [Grove Springs] to stay all night. Had a nice time all day.

Saturday, August 16, 1902
Was at Mother's all day. Uncle Dan, Aunt Emma & Mabel came to stay all night.

Sunday, August 17, 1902
The Perry's went away tonight except Mabel – she stays. Had a pleasant day.

Monday, August 18, 1902
Floyd was sick all day – such a bad cold. I worked on American Beauty doily. At Mother L's.

Tuesday, August 19, 1902
Floyd was up – went fishing. We went over to the Grove Springs House. Mama was there.

Above: Looking west across Keuka Lake toward Bluff Point near Grove Springs. Publisher: The Rotograph Co., NY. Below: The *Mary Bell's* boat landing at the Grove Springs Hotel. Publisher: The Rotograph Co., New York.

Wednesday, August 20, 1902
Went to Keuka tonight on boat. Aunt Sate was up this PM. [She] Went down as far as K [Keuka] with us.

Thursday, August 21, 1902
Mama & I went to Penn Yan on *Mary Bell* and back on it. Called to Estelle's this AM. Floyd came up tonight.

Friday, August 22, 1902
Floyd & I was up home all day. Mama & I went to Keuka and to Wayne with Ned.

Saturday, August 23, 1902
Today was Papa's birthday. We had a nice time. [We] rode down on our wheels to Grove Springs. Mother & I called to Mrs. Floyd Shoemaker's. Poor Floyd had such a tooth ache.

Sunday, August 24, 1902
Floyd went home tonight. I staid to Mother's. It's so lonesome.

Monday, August 25, 1902
Floyd commenced work. I went on *Mary Bell* – met Mama at Keuka. We went to Penn Yan for the ride.

Tuesday, August 26, 1902
I went home with Father L this PM. He drove up after me this PM. Mabel & Carl were at Mother's.

Wednesday, August 27, 1902
Carl & Mabel went on the 7:30 night boat. I am at Mother's.

Thursday, August 28, 1902
I went this PM over to GS [Grove Springs] grounds to the Wixon/Swarthout picnic after 5. I took my wheel for Keuka to Mama's.

Friday, August 29, 1902
Rode down on my wheel this AM. Went to the GS SS picnic. Had a nice time. Went home with Mama on *Mary Bell*.

Saturday, August 30, 1902
Mama & I went to Hport [Hammondsport] to meet Floyd. He came – went back on boat to Mama's. Was so glad to see him.

Sunday, August 31, 1902
Mama & Papa took us to Mother L's in carriage. Aunt Jennie & Leon were there.

Monday, September 1, 1902
We visited all day until 5:30. Took boat for home after such a lovely vacation – arrived here [in Elmira] at 10 PM. Happy as can be.

Tuesday, September 2, 1902
I cleaned up the hall and unpacked the trunk. We rode our wheels to Cora's tonight. Saw the baby.

Wednesday, September 3, 1902
I went downstreet this PM – got draping for the cupboard & 2 towels. Called to Mrs. Mathew's and Mrs. Messinger's. We did not go out this evening.

Thursday, September 4, 1902
I went down to Bundy's this morning – got a basket of peaches. Canned them this PM. We read this PM.

Friday, September 5, 1902
I cleaned up the bath room in AM. Finished Mother BB piece. Esther & Maud Nichols called. It's cool tonight. Did not go out.

Saturday, September 6, 1902
Floyd got home at 4PM. Will Joralemon [of Wayne] came this AM. Staid to dinner with us. Esther & I called to Mrs. J.W. Cleveland's and Mrs. Weygant's. We did not go out tonight.

Sunday, September 7, 1902
We staid home all day. Sat on porch. Read & visited. What a lovely quiet day we had.

Tues. Aug. 26, 1902

I went home with Father L. this P.M. he drove up after me this P.M. Mabel & Carl were at mother's

Wednesday 27

Carl & Mabel went on the 7:30 night boat — I am at mother's

Thursday 28

Went this P.M. over to G.S. grounds to the Mexon Smartout picnic, after 5. I took my wheel for Keuka to Mahan's

Fri. Aug. 29, 1902

Rode down my wheel went to the G.S. S.S. picnic, had a nice time went home with Mama on Mary Bell.

Saturday 30

Mama & I went to H port to meet Floyd. — He came went back on boat to Mama. was so glad to see him —

Sunday 31

Mama & Papa took us to Mother L — in carriage. Aunt Jennie & Leon were there

Sun. Sept. 7, 1902

We staid home all day. Sat on porch, read & visited. What a lovely quiet day we have had.

Monday 8

Floyd went to Office as usual. Will Joralmon was here to dinner. Floyd, Will & I went up to see the K.T. parade. We spent the evening on [?]

Tuesday 9

Floyd went to Office as usual. I ironed. It so cold we did not go out tonight.

Wed. Sept. 10, 1902

Floyd went to O— as usual. I went to depot. Mama did not come. Took our wheels went to Cora Park.

Thursday 11

I am on sick list at 10. Bell W came to dinner. I canned 4 can of peaches. Mama came this 4 P.M. also Mrs Nichols — Mr & Mrs to Roricks

Friday 12

Floyd went to O— as usual. Mama & I went to Matinee was called to Mrs Shoemakers. Tonight took car for Cora to see baby. Boys went to Lodge

Monday, September 8, 1902
Floyd went to office as usual. Will Joralemon was here to dinner. Floyd, Will, & I went up to see the K. J. Parade. We spent the evening over to George & Ella's.

Tuesday, September 9, 1902
Floyd went to office as usual. I ironed. It's so cold we did not go out tonight.

Wednesday, September 10, 1902
Floyd went to office as usual. I went to depot. Mama did not come. Took our wheels – went to Cora Paul's.

Thursday, September 11, 1902
I am on sick list at 10. Belle W came to dinner. I canned 4 cans of peaches. Mama came this 4PM also Mrs. Nichols. We went to Rorick's [Glen].

Friday, September 12, 1902
Floyd went to office as usual. Mama & I went to matinee. We called to Mrs. Shoemaker's. Tonight took car for Cora's to see baby. Boys went to lodge.

Saturday, September 13, 1902
Floyd went to office as usual. Mama & Mrs. Nichols went on 10 AM train for home.

Sunday, September 14, 1902
We went this PM over to Mr. Johnson's on our wheels then Mrs. J took me for a ride. Lillian & Will K called this evening.

Monday, September 15, 1902
Floyd went to office as usual. I went to Hoffman's the florists – got a fern. We went up to Cora's tonight.

Tuesday, September 16, 1902
Floyd went to office as usual. I cleaned up the house. This evening Ella, George, Esther & Mr. Starbird – we went to Alpha Club reception. Then, came here. We had ice cream & wafers.

Wednesday, September 17, 1902

Floyd went to office as usual. I was over to Ella's all the PM. Bake a pumpkin pie this AM. Esther called a little while. We did not go out tonight.

Thursday, September 18, 1902

Floyd went to office as usual. I went downstreet this PM. Called to Esther's. Ella, George & we played poker tonight.

Friday, September 19, 1902

Floyd went to office as usual. I went downstreet this PM. Leon Murdock came at 11 AM. We all went to the Lyceum tonight.

Saturday, September 20, 1902

Floyd went to office as usual. Then he went with Leon to the Reformatory. This PM, Mabel & Josie, Bee K, Ray S, and Mrs. Nichols called.

Sunday, September 21, 1902

Leon, Floyd & I went to church this AM. Ray & Mabel went with us for a trolley ride to Woodlawn [Cemetery] and Rorick's Glen.

Monday, September 22, 1902

Floyd went to office as usual. Leon went home on the 5:20 train. We went to depot with him. We went over to George's a little while tonight.

Tuesday, September 23, 1902

Floyd went to office as usual. I ironed this AM for myself. Helped Ella in PM. We went to Mr. Johnson's. The boys helped him lathe.

Wednesday, September 24, 1902

Floyd went to office as usual. I fussed around all day. Did not go out. Ella & George came over. We played poker.

Thursday, September 25, 1902

Floyd went to office as usual. Bill W came down and spent the day. Esther, Carrie & Mrs. S called. It rains hard tonight.

Friday, September 26, 1902
Floyd went to office as usual. We picked some of the peaches tonight. Ella came over. We played poker.

Saturday, September 27, 1902
I went downstreet to Dr.'s with Esther. Went over to George's – played cards. A pleasant day.

Sunday, September 28, 1902
It rained today. No one came. We read all day and had such a nice quiet day and evening.

Monday, September 29, 1902
Floyd went to office as usual. I finished Mama's BB doily. We walked up to Esther's tonight for a few minutes.

Tuesday, September 30, 1902
Floyd went to office as usual. I pickled some peaches. Worked on rose piece. Mabel P & Ray staid to supper. Rains tonight.

Wednesday, October 1, 1902
Floyd went to office as usual. I spent the whole day with Ella. Mrs. Nichols called. I worked some on my rose piece this evening.

Thursday, October 2, 1902
Floyd went to office as usual. I went downstreet coat hunting. Went to the [Elmira] College to call on Mabel & Joe.

Friday, October 3, 1902
Floyd went to office as usual. Ella, Mrs. Taylor, & I went downstreet this PM. Looked for coat. We went to a Macabee drill at St. James's Hall [former St. Patrick's school at the corner of West Clinton Street and Park Place].

Saturday, October 4, 1902
I am sick list at 9 AM. Floyd went to office as usual. We went downstreet tonight. I bought a Monte Carlo coat.

Tues. Oct. 7, 1902

Floyd went to Office as usual. I ironed this a.m. & cleaned up kitchen. Lillian & Will R— spent the evening here — Had a nice time.

Wednesday 8

Floyd went to Office as usual. I washed kitchen curtains ironed them, put them up. Floyd went to Lodge. Mr & Mrs Roby came for the evening.

Thursday 9

Floyd went to Office as usual. We went to Cora's tonight on car. Mrs Searles came spent the afternoon

Fri. Oct. 10, 1902

Floyd went to Office as usual. Went down St. this P.M. got curtain & for Bath curtain made them this eve — am did not go out

Saturday 11

Floyd went to Office as usual. I made curtain sashes this P.M. and tonight I met with the crowd of the Eastern Star

Sunday 12

Did not get up until 10.30 then went took a car to go over the river, but got off at Water St, I was sick. Geo & Ella called this eve

The Lyceum Theater & Opera House on the corner of Lake and Carroll Streets looking north. On the right is the Gerrity Brothers drugstore.

Sunday, October 5, 1902
Did not get up until 10 AM. Mabel & Ray came – spent the PM. We did not go out. I did not feel well today.

Monday, October 6, 1902
Floyd went to office as usual. I fixed up the kitchen curtains today. Marie Noble called. 2 trays of grapes came this PM. Mr. & Mrs. Emblem called this PM.

Tuesday, October 7, 1902
Floyd went to office as usual. I ironed this AM. I cleaned up the kitchen. Lillian & Will K spent the evening here. Had a nice time.

Wednesday, October 8, 1902
Floyd went to office as usual. I washed kitchen curtains. Ironed them – put them up. Floyd went to lodge. Mr. & Mrs. Roby came for the evening.

Thursday, October 9, 1902
Floyd went to office as usual. We went to Cora's tonight on car. Mrs. Searles came – spent the afternoon.

Friday, October 10, 1902
Floyd went to office as usual. I went downstreet this PM. Got curtain ties for the bath curtains. Made them this evening. We did not go out tonight.

Saturday, October 11, 1902
Floyd went to office as usual. I made curtain sashes this PM and tonight I went with the crowd to the Eastern Star ----. Got home at 1 AM.

Sunday, October 12, 1902
Did not get up until 10:30. Then we took a car to over to the river – got off at Water Street. I was sick. George & Ella called this evening.

Monday, October 13, 1902
Floyd went to office as usual. I was over to Mrs. B---'s – she made my white sleeves smaller. I hemmed the towels. Mabel & Josie called. We did not go out this evening. It thundered and lightninged tonight.

Tuesday, October 14, 1902
Floyd went to office as usual. I was over to Mrs. Ina's a little while. Mr. & Mrs. Mathews came over for the evening.

Wednesday, October 15, 1902
Floyd went to office as usual. I ironed in the AM. Esther, Mrs. Whitman, Mrs. Mathews & Mrs. Nichols called today. Floyd & Mabel & I walked to Lillian's for the evening.

Thursday, October 16, 1902
Floyd went to office as usual. I cleaned the Hall today. Mrs. J washed curtains. We went up to Mrs. Searles's – spent the evening.

Friday, October 17, 1902
Floyd went to office as usual. Started the coal range today. Mabel P came down to stay all night. Ray called. We spent the evening over to Dale's.

Saturday, October 18, 1902
Floyd went to office as usual. I did my mending. Floyd went upstreet tonight – got a hat. It was cold. I did not go out.

Sunday, October 19, 1902
We went to church this AM. Went over to Miss Covill's in PM. Walked both ways. We read this evening. Had a nice time by ourselves.

Monday, October 20, 1902
Floyd went to office as usual. I planted seeds in the yard this PM. Went wheel riding in forenoon. Ella, George, Floyd & I walked to Cora's – spent the evening.

Tuesday, October 21, 1902
Floyd went to office as usual. I ironed in AM. Aunt Sate Knapp Stowell died today. We did not go out this evening.

Wednesday, October 22, 1902

Floyd went to office as usual. Ray & Mabel came down this PM. I went up to Miss Biddleman's. Floyd went to lodge.

Thursday, October 23, 1902

Floyd went to office as usual. I went upstreet to the dressmaker's. We went to the Masonic party at the hall tonight. Had a nice time.

Friday, October 24, 1902

Floyd went to office as usual. I cleaned up the rooms. Aunt Emma & Raymond & Mabel came the PM. Lillian Katzman called. Ray came tonight.

Saturday, October 25, 1902

Floyd went to office as usual. Mother Latier came on the 3:40 train. Having a nice time. Mabel & Aunt Emma here. We went to Eastern Star lodge.

Sunday, October 26, 1902

We did not go to church this AM. Out to Trinity Church this evening. Ray & A. Stapleton called. Mabel staid all night.

Monday, October 27, 1902

Floyd went to office as usual. We went downstreet in AM and to Depot at 1:40. We went to the Fay Magisines [magicians] at the YMCA.

Tuesday, October 28, 1902

Floyd went to office as usual. We visited Lard all day. I did a little ironing & canned one of the pears. Mr. & Mrs. Mathews called tonight.

Wednesday, October 29, 1902

Floyd went to office as usual. We went downstreet – bought Mother a jacket. Called on the girls at the College.

Thursday, October 30, 1902

Floyd went to office as usual. Mother made 25 tumblers of jelly for me. We went to Calvin's, and Cora's & George J's tonight.

From the *Elmira Daily Gazette*, October 29, 1902.

Friday, October 31, 1902
Floyd went to office as usual. I am on sick list. Mabel & Josie, Miss Biddleman & Ray called.

Saturday, November 1, 1902
Floyd went to office as usual. He came down to the depot to see Mother L away. She went at 10 AM. We did not go out tonight. I canned 2 of pears.

Sunday, November 2, 1902
We went to church this AM. Walked up to Cora's & Mrs. Nichols's this PM. Mr. & Mrs. Ina called tonight.

Monday, November 3, 1902
Floyd went to office as usual. I cleaned up the rooms this AM. Walked to office and to Mr. S. We called to Dr. Messinger's this evening.

Tuesday, November 4, 1902
Floyd went to office as usual. Idell for Governor, McCann for Judge we elected. I lost a box of candy betting with Floyd. We went over to George's this evening.

Wednesday, November 5, 1902
Floyd went to office as usual. Miss Biddleman called with my waist I fagoted. I took it up this PM. We did not go out this evening. Mrs. Lewis called.

Thursday, November 6, 1902
Floyd went to office as usual. I cleaned up the house. We went to train – met Father L at depot. I went to Esther's while Floyd went to lodge.

Friday, November 7, 1902
Floyd went to office as usual. This PM went to Binghamton to take shrine. Father & I went to depot with him [Floyd] John came on 3:40 this PM. Esther came.

Saturday, November 8, 1902

Floyd went to office as usual. He arrived on the 4 AM. Had a jolly time. John & I was downstreet most all the day getting his clothes. Miss Noble & Esther came.

Sunday, November 9, 1902

We got up at 9 AM. Ray & Mabel, Esther, Charles Glover called. We went to the Masonic Service at Grace Church this evening. Father, John, Floyd & I had a pleasant time.

Monday, November 10, 1902

Floyd went to office as usual. John & Father L went on train this AM. We went to J. Mathews. They went with us to Jim's for the evening.

Tuesday, November 11, 1902

Floyd went to office as usual. I ironed & mended this PM. We went to Mr. Emblem for evening.

Wednesday, November 12, 1902

Floyd went to office as usual. I mended. Was to Mrs. Messinger's. Floyd went to Lodge for a little while. I staid alone.

Thursday, November 13, 1902

Floyd went to office as usual. I work on Rose centerpiece this PM. We spent the evening at George's with Roby's people.

Friday, November 14, 1902

Floyd went to office as usual. I went downstreet this PM. Got bed room curtains. Mabel & Josie staid all night – their fellows came. Ella came over. Mildred S called.

Saturday, November 15, 1902

Floyd went to office a usual. The girls went about 9:30. I washed windows. Its such a warm day. We went downtown to Berner's after olives.

Sunday, November 16, 1902

We attended church this AM to Baptist church. The girls came down to dinner. Ray let us take his horse to go riding. They staid here. The young people went about 9 PM.

Monday, November 17, 1902

Floyd went to office as usual. I cleaned up in general. We spent the evening at Mr. Shoemaker's.

Tuesday, November 18, 1902

Floyd went to office as usual. I mended some. Ella & I went up to Esther's this PM & downstreet. We went over to Mr. Roby's.

Wednesday, November 19, 1902

Floyd went to office as usual. I ironed & cleaned up. George & Ella came over tonight.

Thursday, November 20, 1902

Floyd went to office as usual. I work some on doily. Papa & Mama came on 3:40 train. Had a pleasant evening.

Friday, November 21, 1902

Floyd went to office as usual. He came down to train & went with Ray to Knights [?] in carriage. Papa & Mama went on 10 AM train. Ella & I went to college this evening.

From the *Elmira Daily Advertiser*, November 25, 1902.

Saturday, November 22, 1902
Floyd went to office as usual. Will & Estelle came on 1:40 train – we did not go out tonight.

Sunday, November 23, 1902
We attended B [Baptist] Church both morning & evening. Went to boarding house for dinner.

Monday, November 24, 1902
Floyd went to office as usual. Stella & I went downstreet this PM. Did not go out this evening. Will went to Bath [New York].

Tuesday, November 25, 1902
Floyd went to office as usual. Stella & I went downstreet this PM. We sate at the table until 8:30. Did not go out tonight.

Wednesday, November 26, 1902
Floyd went to office as usual. It rained all day – so disagreeable. We did not go out. Floyd went to lodge.

Thursday, November 27, 1902
We had a happy Thanksgiving. Estelle & I went to church this AM. Went to boarding house to dinner. Then went to Lyceum "The Christian."

Friday, November 28, 1902
Floyd went to office as usual. Stella & I went downstreet in the PM. I --- my white hat. Lillian & Will K called tonight.

Saturday, November 29, 1902
Floyd went to office as usual. Stella & I changed the rooms around. I cleaned up. Mabel & Joe called today. We all went upstreet tonight.

Sunday, November 30, 1902
I was a little sick all day. Did not go out. Had headache. Ella called this PM.

Mon. Nov. 24, 1902

Floyd went to office as usual. Stella & I went down street this P.M., did not go out this eve. Will Mr & Bath.

Tuesday 25

Floyd went to office as usual. Stella & I went down St. this P.M. — we sat at the table until 8.30, did not go out tonight.

Wednesday 26

Floyd went to office as usual. It rained all day, so disagreeable. We did not go out. Floyd went to Lodge.

Thurs. Nov. 27, 1902

We had a happy Thanksgiving. Estelle & I went to church this a.m., went to boarding house to dinner, then when to the Lyceum. The Christian

Friday 28

Floyd went to office as usual. Stella & I went down St. in the P.M. I ironed my white Wat. Lillian & Will K— called tonight.

Saturday 29

Floyd went to office as usual. Stella & I changed the rooms around & cleaned up. Mabel & Jos. called today. We all went up St. tonight.

Monday, December 1, 1902
Floyd went to office. Stella made a pie. Will to Bath as usual. I went to depot – Aunt Emma & Jennie to the 10AM. Mabel & Ray were here this evening. We had a nice time. Stella slept with me.

Tuesday, December 2, 1902
Floyd went to office as usual. I went this AM to the cut glass factory with Aunt. Then Stella & I went to depot to see them off at 5:20. We did not go out this evening. Floyd went to lodge.

Wednesday, December 3, 1902
Floyd went to office as usual. I ironed, but went first to depot with Estelle. We spent the evening home. Ella & George came over.

Thursday, December 4, 1902
Floyd went to office as usual. Ella & I went downstreet this PM. Stella & Will came at 10 tonight. Floyd went to lodge.

Friday, December 5, 1902
Floyd went to office as usual. He wore boots the snow was so deep. It's a beautiful cold day. We did not go out.

Saturday, December 6, 1902
Floyd went to office as usual. Estelle & I went downstreet this PM. Bought Lizzie seiley(?) for her wedding present. Floyd went to Macabee Lodge. Mrs. Ina came over – played cards with Will, Estelle & I.

Sunday, December 7, 1902
We all went to Baptist Church & Sabbath School. Joe & Mabel called this PM. Will visited us over to dinner this noon. We did not go out this evening.

Monday, December 8, 1902
Floyd went to office as usual. It is a terrible cold day. We went downstreet. Stella bought me a salad bowl.

Tuesday, December 9, 1902

Floyd went to office as usual. Stella went downstreet toward night. Went to Reynolds Brothers. Will J went away today to Keuka. We 3 went to the play "The Great White Diamond." It was grand.

Wednesday, December 10, 1902

Floyd went to office as usual. Stella & I ironed. Esther, Clinton & Cora called. We went calling this PM to the college and I went to H. Chapman's to 3rd Street. Floyd went to a banquet.

Thursday, December 11, 1902

Floyd went of office as usual & to lodge tonight. It snowed all day but Stella & I went to the Industrial Fair. Will J came home this evening.

Friday, December 12, 1902

Floyd went to office as usual. Stella & I went downstreet. I bought lots of Xmas gifts. Floyd went to lodge. Mr. & Mrs. Be---, Ella & Mrs. Mathews came tonight.

Saturday, December 13, 1902

Floyd went to office as usual. He wore boots – the snow is high. Will & Floyd went upstreet tonight. I am making Esther's apron.

Sunday, December 14, 1902

We did not go to church. Out this PM. We all went up on West Second Street to look at house. We staid to supper with the Pauls then went to church.

Monday, December 15, 1902

Floyd went to office as usual. Estelle went downstreet. I bought 3 books at the auction. It is a dark day. We are so tired.

Tuesday, December 16, 1902

Floyd went to office as usual. Stella & I went downstreet this PM. Finished Esther's apron this PM. We did not go out this evening.

Wednesday, December 17, 1902
Floyd went to office as usual. Stella & I went downstreet this PM. Then Floyd & I went down tonight to get Mrs. J a picture.

Thursday, December 18, 1902
Floyd went to office as usual. I started on 10 AM train for Penn Yan. Arrived home at 3:30 – walked up the hill. Floyd went to lodge.

Friday, December 19, 1902
Floyd went to office as usual. Papa went to Penn Yan. Mama & I staid alone & visited. Had a nice time. I went on the boat to Grove [Springs]. Staid all night to Mother's [Latier?]

Saturday, December 20, 1902
Father L took me up home. Mama & I spent the day alone – had a nice visit. Received a letter from Floyd that his salary was advanced to 90.00 in January.

Sunday, December 21, 1902
We had a nice visit today. It was a stormy day. Lonesome without Floyd.

Monday, December 22, 1902
Papa & Mama went to Hport [Hammondsport] today. I staid home with the boys.

Tuesday, December 23, 1902
Papa & Mama & I went to Penn Yan on boat. Met Floyd at train. Spent the evening at my house. I was so glad to see Floyd.

Wednesday, December 24, 1902
The boys went hunting. Floyd's gun exploded – so fortunate he was not injured. This PM Papa & Mama took us to Father Latier's.

Thursday, December 25, 1902
Papa, Mama & the boys all came to Mother L's for our Merry Xmas dinner. What a happy day we all had. We came to Elmira tonight. Found everything nice.

Wed. Dec. 24, 1902

The boys went hunting Floyd gun exploded so fortunate he was not injured. this P.M. Papa & Mama took us to Father Later's

Thursday 25

Papa Mama & the boys all came to Mother & gave us Merry X mas dinner what a happy day we all had. we came to Elmira tonight everything nice

Friday 26

Floyd went to Office as usual this morning Estella & I went down St then I went to Office saw Mr. S— came back with Floyd we all went over to Ella's tonight

Sat. Dec. 27, 1902

Floyd went to Office as usual. Lillian K— & Ella J— called this P.M. Floyd & I went to Evening Star Lodge

Sunday 28

We stood up late until quite late did not go to church but we all went to the Cantata at Lake St. Presbyterian church this eve—

Monday 29

Floyd went to Office until 3— then he went to Binghamton with the "Shriners" Stella & I went to the depot and called on Esther Miss Noble, & Mrs. F. Sunday

Friday, December 26, 1902
Floyd went to office as usual this morning. Estelle & I went downstreet – then I went to office saw Mrs. S [Stowell]. Came back with Floyd. We all went over to Ella's tonight.

Saturday, December 27, 1902
Floyd went to office as usual. Lillian K. & Ella J called this PM. Floyd & I went to Evening Star Lodge.

Sunday, December 28, 1902
We staid in bed until quite late. Did not go to church but we all went to the Cantata at Lake Street Presbyterian church this evening.

Monday, December 29, 1902
Floyd went to office until 3 – then he went to Binghamton with the "shriners." Stella & I went to the depot and called on Esther, Miss Noble, & Mrs. F. Sunderlin.

Tuesday, December 30, 1902
Floyd went to office as usual. Ella & I called to Walkers, Pickleys, Mattico, Katie Burdick, etc this PM. Mr. & Mrs. Mathews were here tonight. Floyd went to George's to audit his books – they went upstreet.

Wednesday, December 31, 1902
Floyd went to office as usual. Stella & Will went home for a visit on 10 AM train. I swept the bedroom – cleaned up in general. We have spent a happy year. God grant [that] we may have many more.

Ther.　　Tues. Dec. 30, 1902　　Wea.

Floyd went to office
as usual. Ella & I called
re Walkers, Pickleys, Matties, Kitty
Benedicts etc &ther P.M.
Mr & Mrs Mathews move
here to night —
Floyd went to George's
to audit his books, then
went up St.

Ther.　　Wednesday 31　　Wea.

Floyd went to office
as usual.
Stella & Will went
home for a visit on
10 a.m. train.
I swept the bed
room cleaned up in
general. We have
spent a happy
year. God grant
we may have
many more.

Afterward

Floyd died in 1926. In 1929 Emma went to Europe. The passenger list said she was 53 and lived in Wayne, New York. She sailed home on the S.S. Montrose. The 1930 census showed she lived in Wayne, New York with her parents on Road Number 1.

In April 1952, Emma moved into the Pleasant View Hospital, 510 Fitch Street in Elmira - across the street from the Arnot- Ogden Memorial Hospital.

Emma died in 1955 in Elmira and was buried beside her husband in the Tyrone Union Cemetery, Cemetery Road, in Tyrone, New York.

An image in the back of Emma's diary.

Bibliography

Ancestry.com. Border Crossings: From Canada to U.S., 1895-1956 [database on-line]. Provo, UT, USA: Ancestry.com Operations Inc, 2008.

Penn Yan Chronicle Express, April 3, 1952, page 7, "Wayne."

Year: 1930; Census Place: Wayne, Steuben, New York; Roll 1649; Page: 1B; Enumeration District: 77; Image: 518.0.

http://www.rootsweb.ancestry.com/~nyschuyl/tyuncem1.htm

More *Learning From History* publications from
New York History Review Press

A Darned Good Time
by Miss Lucy Potter, 1868

My Centennial Diary - A Year in the Life of a Country Boy by Earll K. Gurnee, 1876

My Story - A Year in the Life of a Country Girl
by Ida Burnett, 1880

Home in These Hills
by Viola Coolbaugh, 1891

www.ingramcontent.com/pod-product-compliance
Lightning Source LLC
Chambersburg PA
CBHW051708040426
42446CB00008B/777